GHOSTS OF GLAMORGAN
PART TWO

Author: Karl-James Langford

Ghosts of Glamorgan
Part Two of a series of books that discusses first-hand account stories from Glamorgan's ghostly past

Author:
Karl-James Langford FSAScot, MLitt

Artwork:
Michelle Harrhy

Archaeology Cymru Media
Copyright 2021 ©

First Edition (Impression 1)
Published by **Archaeology Cymru Media**
Publisher No. 698848
ISBN-13: 978 0952939498
ISBN-1-0952939495
Retail Price: **£11.99**

Printed by:
Integrated Graphics Ltd
Units 8 and 9
Palmerston Workshops
Palmerston Road
Barry
Vale of Glamorgan
CF63 2YZ

Author can be contacted directly on:
karljlangford@hotmail.com
or Tel: 07437 747402

PART TWO in a series of books that discusses first-hand account stories from Glamorgan's ghostly past

PLACES WE VISIT IN THIS EDITION
There is NO order to the items we discuss,
each one drags you in to read another:

Aberthaw	Lavernock
Bargoed	Marcross
Barry	Merthyr Mawr
Cardiff	North Cornelly
Culverhouse Cross (Cardiff)	Penarth
Cog (Sully)	Penrhys
Cowbridge	Peterston-super-Ely
Dinas Powys	Porth
Ebbw Vale	Rhoose
Ewenny	St. Athan
Gileston	St. Hilary
Llanblethian	Tinkinswood
Llandaff	Tylorstown
Llandough	Wenvoe
Llanmihangel	West Aberthaw
Llantwit Major	Wick

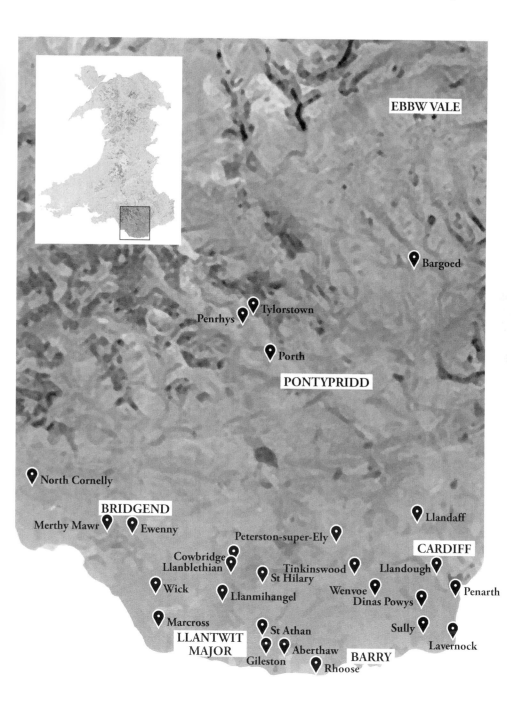

STORY INDEX

A Ghost At The Boys Village | St. Athan   12

The Lavernock Ghost | Lavernock   14

Our First Visit To Bronwydd Park | Porth   18

The RAF Airman | Rhoose   22

Warning Of The Gwrach | Penarth   26

The Unfulfilled Restless Spirit Of Wick | Wick   30

A Cog House With A Mysterious Wailing Child | Cog   32

Tinkinswood Burial Chamber | Tinkinswood   36

The Lady Of The Well At The Duke Of Wellington | Cowbridge   40

The Death Dog Of Dimlands Road | Llantwit Major   44

A Ghost Story Linked To The Second World War | St. Athan   46

A Ghost At Penrhys Speaks | Penrhys   50

Time Travel To Be Avoided | Ewenny   54

The Wood Wose Beast Of Peterston-Super-Ely | Peterston-Super-Ely   58

The Boys Village At West Aberthaw | Aberthaw   62

A Bronwydd Park Ghost Story | Porth   64

St. Quintin's Castle A Vision From The Past | Llanblethian   66

Haunted House | Cardiff   68

A Very Barry Ghost Story, Burlington Street | Barry   74

Marcross Medieval Church, A New Look On An Old Story | Marcross   76

78	The Amertyville Story Of Dinas Powys	Dinas Powys
80	Events At Tylorstown	Tylorstown
84	A New Insight Into A Ghost	Merthyr Mawr
88	The Spirit At The Lay-By	Llanmihangel
90	A Story Of Footsteps	Llandaff North
92	A Ghost In A Trailer Culverhouse Cross	Cardiff
94	A Story Of A Phantom Wedding	Cowbridge
96	North Cliff Dock Beach	Penarth
98	The Fate Of Billy Parrock	Gileston
104	A Roman Ghost	Llandough
106	A Ghost Walking At RAF St Athan	St Athan
108	The Burtons Ghost Of Bargoed Part I	Bargoed
112	A Pixie And The Great Grandparents	North Cornelly
116	A Ghost In The Room	Aberthaw
120	Wenvoe Nursing Home	Wenvoe
122	An Entity	Penrhys
126	The Roman Road	St. Hilary
128	The Burtons Ghost Of Bargoed Part II	Bargoed
130	The Church Ghost	Cowbridge
134	More Ghosts From Penrhys	Penrhys
138	The Story Of Elm Grove Road	Dinas Powys
142	Things That Happen: An Item That Was Meant To Arrive	St Athan
144	A Recorded Voice	Ewenny

STORY CONTRIBUTORS:

Abby

Alex Morgan

Ceri-Elaine Barnes

Dean Drakes

Denis Doyle

Donna Pennington

Emma Jenkins

Huw Trivett

James Eddy

James Wilcock

Jane, Jeffrey

Martin Davies

Michael Austin

Nathan Williams

Nigel Nash

Randy Mandy McCourt

Richard Enos

Rosamund

Sarah

Simon Jenkins

Steve

The Lad

The Raven

Life is very rarely ever about what we want to achieve, you can never seek out ghosts, for those ghosts only ever find us.

Sometimes in life our direction and path are set very much by what we wish to achieve. One of those achievements was never to write any books on ghosts, but this is my second outing in that genre. A genre that has been set by those I have met, and circumstance that has developed around me. Very much this short entry of mine, is truly much about those ghosts that we can occasionally find that seek us out.

This book has been greatly inspired by the love and dedication of Michelle, and without her, I would not be the person I am today. For Michelle has created, and seen that opportunity for me every step of the way over the past 6 years and more.

We won't undertake a lengthy introduction, we want you to simply get to the stories. But how about this for a start? Picture a white figure with no legs that had gone across the road right, in front of Nigel and went down the little lane. This had been at a brisk pace to avoid traffic. Where is this ghost being seen? You need to read on.

I did have other stories for this book, but hey we couldn't use everything. So, there is a book three on the cards, but you may be waiting a few years for that as I have a load more projects I need to get into print.

So, thanks for taking the time to purchase this book, enjoy and read on. Many kind wishes, and may this book last the test of time.

Karl-James Langford FSAScot, MLitt
Fellow of the Society of Scottish Antiquaries
Master of Letters Degree with the University of Highlands and Islands
Post Graduate Diploma in Archaeology and Heritage University of Leicester

GHOSTS OF GLAMORGAN

PART TWO

A GHOST AT THE BOYS VILLAGE

ST. ATHAN

The land at the Boys Village to be precise West Aberthaw, will be developed shortly, and all but one of the buildings, the 'War memorial' will be removed. But before the construction of the 'Boys Village' in the 1920s, this was the haunt of smugglers and traders throughout the ages.

This is an amazing story, that needs to be told. This was originally a story verbally told by Abby to us and written down by her friend Emma. Abby and her dad went to view one of the buildings at the St. Athan Boys village; with a view to doing it up. There had been a small number of red brick houses for sale.

When they got there, the door was open, so they went inside to have a quick nose round. It's human nature to be nosey. Whilst having a look, a man appeared, it seemed from nowhere. Odd that they both thought they didn't hear a car pull up. The man just suddenly seemed to appear behind them, and they didn't hear anyone approaching.

"Hey ho". they both thought lets get on with the viewing. He had a blue suit on, and he started showing them round and telling them about the building. Then when it was time to go upstairs, he said he was going to go ahead, and he'd be back for them in a minute. They waited for ages and ages, and he didn't come back down, so they went upstairs to investigate; what was taking so long? They started looking in each of the rooms, but they couldn't see the man.

They were in the last room and there was no sign of the man, but he suddenly appeared behind them again. They didn't hear him approach, yet again. They carried on the viewing and went back downstairs. They walked outside, and the man said he just had to lock up and he'd be out in a minute.

They waited again for a while and a car drove up. An estate agent got out and said he was there to do the viewing, which confused Abby and her dad. The estate agent said he had the only set of keys, and when they tried the door, it was locked. They didn't want the place after that and left.

What an amazing story. Moral, get out to the Boys Village, and its surrounding housing, before it is all demolished.

THE LAVERNOCK GHOST

LAVERNOCK

The site of military importance in the Second World War, that was home to a full gun battery, original being placed into service in 1870.

The event unfolded at the Lavernock Second World War battery near Sully (Vale of Glamorgan), around 6 years ago; a sunny summer day around 3pm, plenty of light. Nathan and 'the lad', were having a father and son photo shoot, on the far side of the battery.

Having looked at the digital images at home, there was a World War Two soldier wearing a distinctive 'British bull helmet', standing 10ft behind 'the lad'; he was a slight individual not a large over fed soldier - the same build as the author. At the time Nathan informs us that there was no feeling of heaviness or activity, a pleasant summer day.

But 'the lad' remembered however feeling a tiny bit cold. The 'lad' remembered more details about the soldier's nose and head, than the rest of the image. Having gone back there again the brace of father and son, although recreating the moment, were unable to reproduce an image of the ghost.

OUR FIRST VISIT TO BRONWYDD PARK

A SENSING DOG IN PORTH

Porth is a historic town that owes most of its existence to mining. By the Victorian period it had become a thriving town of the good and godly- it's chapels.

Huw Trivett tells us of an eerie experience during an evening jaunt with his dog in Porth Park. It was a grey overcast November evening, with a touch of rain in the air, hunched up against the cold, Huw wearily tracked the dog's footsteps as he scampered down the hill. Expecting him to carry on straight for town to sniff around the shop doorways, but he inexplicably turned to flight, heading into the darkness of the park. Why? Even in the day a walk in the park is not for him.

Grudgingly wearily trundling along the crumbling paths, he will follow Huw, but on this evening the dog would rather be in the lead. He would rather be out in front passing through the ever-open park gates; the dog soon disappeared into the gloom, barely visible in the faint moonlight. A moonlight that struggled to peep through the mesh of tangled and twisted branches that loomed overhead. But Huw could hear him as he scrambled through the mass of dead grass and brown gnarled bracken. Well, Huw hoped it was him. Something brushed Huw's leg that must have been him. What else could it have been?

Huw had never been afraid of the dark; having played in a supposed haunted house in his youth, but now that eerie feeling came over Huw as he approached the desolate and unused band stand. Surprisingly it had stood the test of time, with little sign of real wear and tear, though a fresh coat of paint would not go amiss; but it is not a welcoming place, certainly not at night. The band stand is sat overlooking a semi-circle of ruined moss-covered concrete benches, it emits a strange and creepy aura. And Huw can now well believe that people predisposed to physic phenomena, could well feel the presence of a ghostly audience. Huw certainly did.

The dog seemed to sense Huw's unease, or he was just bored with the uninteresting surroundings, as to Huw's relief he now headed out of the park and down to the lights of the town. Huw followed at a brisk pace, glad to be away, vowing never to return at night or even on a miserable gloomy day. Would you?

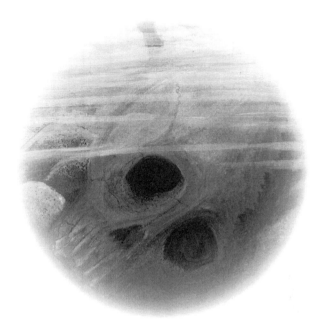

THE RAF AIRMAN

RHOOSE

Fonmon sits quietly in the beating heart of the Vale of Glamorgan. The original castle at Fonmon dates to the early 1100s, parts of the original masonry still exist, with walls up to 5ft in width. The village still retains its pond.

Donna Pennington tells us her story. Her family moved into Fonmon Park Road in Rhoose Porthkerry in April 2015. A lovely house situated between countryside and beach. The house had not been occupied for some time and needed some TLC. Donna had always been able to see spirits, ghosts. As soon as her family moved in she had this feeling that there was definitely something there. The air smelt funny and at first put it down to the house being cold, and did not think no more about it.

They settled in and Donna started getting this vivid picture in her mind of an RAF airman. The picture was so vivid, as she'd not got anyone in the forces it had to be something else. Her family could definitely feel cold spots in the living-room even though it was summer. They started to see fingerprints, like someone had rubbed their fingers across the patio doors. They were not Donna's and not her husbands. They also started smelling very strong cigarette smoke. Donna is a non-smoker and so is her husband, this smell was like woodbine or capstan as her husband said.

Donna was getting more pictures and she said to her husband an RAF AIRMAN is still here. She could feel the air, which was heavy with this smell, we also started to smell oil like petrol. They do not have a car, nevertheless the smell was in the house. She started to get more pictures of this airman, he was tall and an officer. He had a jacket on and a dark hair moustache. The man also had a black Labrador; we started seeing our own dog suddenly get up and run across the living-room. We even heard what could be described as a sharp slap and paw noises on the kitchen floor, and there was no one in there on inspection.

Donna's husband who is not a believer, even though he knew Donna could see spirits. He was sceptical, but even he started to say there's definitely something here. Then one day Donna's husband was videoing on her mobile phone and noticed cats staring, she yelled to my husband, "come see this." I had heard of orbs, but this was unbelievable and definitely not dust. There were blue/yellow flashing orbs coming out of the walls and out of the mirrors.

They watched and one come right down the stairs. Was this our airman or had they come across something more. Since then, they see these orbs outside and they see them in the bedrooms. Also, the TV has gone on at night, and windows open when they have been closed.

There was one night that the bedroom door opened, and a tall man was there, exactly how Donna described. Donna does not get scared but seeing this man like this, Donna woke her husband. Donna has felt a cold breath on her as well. Donna has also had pictures of a large plane crash here and this RAF man walk out. This is the first time Donna has written about this, they are trying to investigate the history of the area. They do know the RAF were stationed there at St. Athan, they do know ports in Barry were used for sailing to D Day landings destinations. What they know is there's definitely an RAF airman's ghost in their house. When her friends have been shown pictures of orbs, some have said they can see a tall man.

These occurrences happen at night and only Donna and her husband live there. Their daughter who had come to stay on holiday also had an experience as well with her young baby son. She felt something in the room and did smell cigarette smoke too.

People will be sceptical, and Donna does come from a family that do see spirits. "My great grandfather was a medium. All I know from the minute they moved in, this airman officer made himself known. Maybe he didn't like having people here, as its had a few tenants who didn't stay long." Donna asked her neighbour and they have not seen anything. So that is the story.

There's too much happened in the house to be make believe, they have pictures of the orbs so you can make your own mind up. Donna and her husband are not planning on sending him on his way, they live there so he will just need to live with them, till he decides to go on or they do.

WARNING OF THE GWRACH

PENARTH

The Gwrach y Rhibyn, is the hideous winged hag of a witch that arrives, with a potent of doom; it may take your life or that of a loved one.

Dreams of the Gwrach y Rhibyn, in Penarth told to us by the Raven. Over two years ago my friend's son's wife lost a baby. I had a dream the night before, that the father of my friend's husband was smiling at me whilst holding 'the baby' at the Railway Inn, Penarth, and was saying to me, "I've thrown down the Gwrach; look I'm holding the baby and the baby is happily with me". But I woke up the next day, and realised the powerful meaning of the dream. My friend did in fact very tragically lose her baby, but it had been protected whilst on the way to the afterlife by its very own grandfather.

It is highly un-usual in the genre of the Gwrach y Rhibyn, to be put in her place in this type of way. There is very little you can do to stop the Gwrach, but on this occasion the granddad had the power to protect the baby. The Gwrach y Rhibyn did not take away the child's life force.

THE UNFULFILLED RESTLESS SPIRIT OF WICK

WICK

The spirits of many souls wander the village of Wick, with its links to wreckers at the coast, there is no wonder we visit Wick here. The ghosts of these wreckers must haunt it's two remaining inns: Lamb and Flag and The Star.

James tells us that he lives in a 3-bedroom house along St. Brides Road, Wick was built in the 1950s. James tells us that there had never been a bad feeling around the place, but there have been a few strange things happen. Mainly these 'happenings' are about seeing something out of the corner of your eye, or could that be anything?

The previous owners of the house were an elderly couple, the man went into hospital for an ingrowing toenail which got infected. This infection led to the gentleman having his leg amputated so the council built an extension for him to be able to get a wheelchair round including a wet room. Unfortunately, tragedy struck, the very unfortunate man never came home, and died in hospital. The wet room is where the strangest event has happened in the house; and more than once. The door is an extra wide heavy door big enough to get a wheelchair through. When it is closed there is no way for the door can open without turning the handle.

James and his wife were sat down with their 4 children eating and watching TV in their front room, when they all heard a high-pitched squeak. The door handle slightly turned, and the door opened about 2 feet and stopped. There had been no one in the wet room, but James felt the hair on the back of his neck stand on end and a shiver went down his spine. There have been a quite a few occasions where the door has been closed, when you leave the room and when you come back in it is open.

James wonders if it is the previous owner trying to get some use out of the wet room he never saw or used in life? I believe truly the door should be left open when not in use, and the gentleman would like it to be that way. It may also be a warning; the door may need to be open one day when there is an emergency!

A COG HOUSE WITH A MYSTERIOUS WAILING CHILD

COG, SULLY

The small hamlet of Cog, sits on a crossroads. Go South you reach Swanbridge and Lavernock, head West you reach Sully, and North you are on a one-way ticket for Cogan Hall, or Dinas Powys. There is large Model farm complex from the 1840s or there about, and the hamlet contains a foray of buildings that pre-date the 1900s.

Nathan tells us he was undertaking with a colleague some electrical work at a farmhouse building, at Cog, near Sully. It's located opposite the turning for Swanbridge, if you turn right and go up the folk in the road you will be adjacent to the well on the green. The project we were involved in, was in that white building on the right-hand side of the road.

The house was unoccupied, the owners were away at the time. After he had started work on the electrics, Nathan shortly went out to the van to get some 'bits and pieces', and to his amazement the Astra van started rocking side to side. I thought it was my colleague messing around, but he hadn't left the house as he was wiring up, after I had left for the van. Then I went back out to the van, on my hands and knee's looking for screws, at the rear of the vehicle it started rocking back and forth yet again. I confronted my colleague to ask why he was messing about several times, and he said it was not him.

I was then using an old corded drill; one that you plug into the mains; on the hammer facility for drilling masonry. The sound was of whining, a white noise over the sound of the drill. But this incredibly wasn't the only noise.

Above the sound of the drilling, there was the sound of a child crying upstairs. As soon as the finger was placed off the trigger, the sound of the crying had gone. Remember the house was un-occupied at the time, so you can image this was pretty hair raising.

Nathan later finds out that there is a history of something happening to children in the farmhouse.

TINKINSWOOD BURIAL CHAMBER

A FEELING IN TINKINSWOOD

Tinkinswood Burial Chamber; so, called, may not have started off as a burial chamber. In fact, Professor Colin Richards (University of the Highlands and Islands) believes that these Neolithic structures in general; constructed as far back as 6,000 years ago (and in some cases more), were only used for burial in their final years of use. Tinkinswood, is just north of Dyffryn and South of St. Nicholas, and holds the record as having one of the biggest capstones on a chamber in Britain at a whopping 50 tonnes.

Having organised several ghostly evening walks at Tinkinswood with Ghost Experience Cymru, I thought it fitting to share two stories.

On the night of Friday December 4th, 2020 that is 3 individuals; of a group of over a dozen witnesses the following: We proceeded with the stories heading up to the chamber, one being of Meyrick, the others of the archaeological work, other chambers and so on. After going through the gate that leads to the chamber, we offered an entertaining history of the site, and nothing unusual about that. After a photo shoot, we headed to leave the enclosed area by the gate.

Our Steward Jeff, myself and one other experienced a feeling of nausea just before leaving via the gate into the open field in front of the Tinkinswood Burial property. Backing onto the tree's behind in my case, looking towards the gate, I had an intense feeling of being sick, and a headache. The same description was from the other two. Why this is the case has not yet been defined.

Also, the second offering is this. In late 2016, I undertook another ghost walk. It was one of those evenings I was very open about my faith, and it shocked everyone, but we carried on. After saying goodbye to everyone at the small car park, I spoke to Michelle on the phone; and told her I was going back to the chamber. She asked me not to go back; it was part of my OCD to go and have a quick look before leaving.

About a year previous, we had spread a friend's ashes at the chamber, and I think this has a link with the following. As I headed towards the chamber of a dank dark atmospheric evening, there it was, a white figure hovering the Tinkinswood chamber. To say I was scared and shocked is an understatement. I approached, and opened the gate into the property, and the figure disappeared. I could not see any features. But to this day I would describe the figure as tall, medium build and the feeling it was looking at me, although I could not see features. What I felt was it must have been the ghost of my friend.

With these stories, I would say Tinkinswood is magical at night, ghosts or not, get there.

THE LADY OF THE WELL AT THE DUKE OF WELLINGTON

COWBRIDGE

The Duke of Wellington (Vale of Glamorgan) was once known as the Black Horse amongst other names. Built facing the original Roman street, it stands to reason that the well to the rear of the premisses is of Roman period date.

Rosamund went with her daughter and grandson Stav to the Duke of Wellington on a February afternoon for lunch in 2019. This was a stopover for her daughter buying a wedding dress. We all sat at a table near the well to the rear of the establishment. We chatted and had our lunch. We were invited to look at the hall to the rear of the 'Duke', to see if this could have been appropriate for a wedding reception.

So eventually Charlotte and Stav put on their coats getting ready to leave, and Rosamund looked up. She was startled to see a lady stood at the table, by the well, dressed in all grey 'completely grey'. So, she said to Charlotte and Stav did you see that lady, and they said no, and carried on out of the establishment. Then as Rosamund was leaving she read the story of the grey lady on the wall, but nobody had told her about the grey lady before the visitation. Talking to the man at the bar with black hair and dark eyes very helpful, asked about history of the place, they were busy.

Totally unexpected it was the afternoon; having lunch, it was the normal mundane lunch, but with the excitement of purchasing the dress.

The Duke of Wellington is full of history at atmospheric for a place to have lunch, with the well. That may have been originally in the courtyard outside in the Romans and Medieval periods, now it is inside, all lit up. Sit by the well, with your mates or family.

How lonely would the grey lady have been in lock-down when the Duke was closed. Did she visit Rosamund, due to the positive energies of the buying the wedding dress, a family occasion? Did the Grey Lady trouble Rosamund, although a little startled in a positive way not expecting a lady at the table. This was a quiet slight standing women, ephemeral, slim, in long silvery spider bluey grey colour old fashioned clothes. The loose wispy fitting type of affair of clothes allowed our Grey lady to almost glide around. The heading covering is of a medieval maid Marian like. She was also shorter than Rosamund at around 4ft 9inches, and definitely a woman and not a girl. The Grey Lady gave the appearance of being a proud lady, that was very clever, not pompous just all knowing.

Rosamund tells us that the moment was so fast, the Grey Lady didn't linger. Rosamund wanted to say hello, but the lady was gone. An observing ghost, for a nice occasion with a family having lunch.

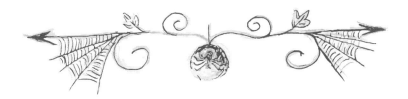

THE DEATH DOG OF DIMLANDS ROAD

LLANTWIT MAJOR

Dimlands Road, is the main access road between Llantwit Major and St. Donat's, heading in a Westerly direction.

The Dimlands Road, Llantwit Major (Vale of Glamorgan), is abound with stories of phantoms, and often I am asked, about its mysteries. This is just a short insert in the book, but worth it.

Donna Pennington, recants the following. "In school we were told that if you saw the big dog with the red eyes on Dimlands Road then you would die." This is a familiar story, for what Donna is discussing here is the Black Shuck, that is part of the folk law across villages throughout Glamorgan. These big black dogs with flaming red eyes, if seen by a mortal, prepare to meet thy doom. Llysworney is one such place in the Vale of Glamorgan that the dog is so much in presence. However, has anyone lived to tell the story?

Donna tells us that, "we used to walk up there purposely in the dark looking for it!!!" Well in this case Donna didn't find the big dog with the red eyes, as she lived to tell the story of her search.

A GHOST STORY LINKED TO THE SECOND WORLD WAR

ST. ATHAN

RAF St. Athan began as a military base commencing in 1936 as a response to the build-up of German forces, before the actual breakout of war on 1st September 1939. My very own Grandad Noah Langford was involved in the construction of the base, where stories of him on a dumper truck moving spoil onto their roofs.

James Eddy offers us an intriguing story. Whilst on gate guard in the Royal Air Force at St Athan, James got talking to an RAF military policeman. The policeman who told James that a few months earlier he was out on a mobile patrol driving around the camp, when he saw someone walking on the road around the runway.

The man on the runway, he said looked like he was wearing Second World War flying clothing; and thought he must be one of the officers from the mess who may had been to a fancy-dress party.

So, the policeman decided to turn round and give him a lift back to the officer's mess. The man in the 'flying cloths' didn't say anything at all on the short journey from East to West camp, the policeman drove round the front of the mess and stopped.

The man got out of the Land Rover, then the policeman said goodbye, and turned the vehicle round to drive off. But in the short space of time the man had disappeared. It was only when he got back to the camp police section and spoke to a couple of the other police officers. A couple of the officers said that the same thing had happened to them, and others over the years. That is when the military policeman had then realised that the man must have been one of the many pilots stationed there during the war. At any one time there were up to 14,000 personnel of all description based at RAF St. Athan.

A GHOST AT PENRHYS SPEAKS

PENRHYS

In the 1960s, there were reports after reports of monastic remains being uncovered by workmen across the Penrhys Housing Estate construction site. Alas, it was the developer's instructions to all its worker's, not to stop work for any archaeological discoveries. Human remains, and fine dress stone have been reported as being dis-guarded and destroyed. So, it is no reason that this former consecrated ground offers us so many ghosts.

Dean Drakes offers us another rich nugget of a story. Dean lived at the Penrhys estate in the late 1970s and early 1980s, a place he loved, but against a dark backdrop. This story was related to Dean in around 1978 or 1979 by John McPhail, who was the Policeman at Penrhys. John McPhail was the resident Policeman for Penrhys, also more relevant to this story he was also a sub lieutenant in the sea-cadets, alongside Dean who was a sea-cadet. Dean tells us, "We used to have a chat during a free period (what you call a stand easy), and we talked about all sorts. John had a nickname on Penrhys; known as 'copper John'."

The subject of ghosts was told to me and a few others. Copper John used to live in one of the old police houses on the estate. Because there had been a small police station up there at the time. Whilst he was off duty, copper John woke up one night in the early hours and to his utter surprise there was a monk stood in the corner of his bedroom. A dark hooded figure! He just looked at it, it didn't say or do anything, just stood there, and slowly faded away, dissipating into nothing. He felt terrified, copper John hadn't told many people due to the fear of being ridiculed.

Dean believes that the entity must have been associated with the old monastery at Penrhys. Dean's own thoughts, thinking as a paranormal; he visualised back to that original conversation with John McPhail, and he could see that the monk was wearing a belt, and that the monks' arms had been down by his side, with his feet in some kind of sandals. The habit had wide sleeves, with a very big hood. But there is something very unusual about Dean's thoughts of the conversation, if it was a Cistercian monk, he describes a leather type belt and a big buckle. Regular monks didn't have buckles? The mystery continues. He believed that copper John, had looked at the entity for 10 minutes. Had there been Cistercian monks, he thought?

As the author of this book, a dew point of fact is that many people had seen things at Penrhys, I don't think the policeman would have been ridiculed; as this is one of many similar reports I have heard about the estate.

The old police station, which is a small building with parking, just off Heol Pendyrus still exists (nearly opposite the cemetery and school) is now converted into housing. And one of two purpose-built police houses where copper John lived is close by.

TIME TRAVEL TO BE AVOIDED

EWENNY

Ewenny takes the visitor to a world of deceit and lies. The South and North gatehouses, are a lot more than an entrance or an exit into a monastic complex. This is a place of a great deal of military important in the medieval period. Such high walls, and gateways to guard a hand full of monks and an abbot, think again. The ghosts haunt every step of the way at Ewenny.

As part of a haunted evening way back in early 2020 we visited the Southern very little visited gateway of the Ewenny Priory. It was a routine exercise to sense any presence, the perception of sound, light, sense, or sight, we had some basic detecting equipment.

After a discussion underneath the arch of the South gatehouse; where there was plenty of light, I felt neutral, no negative energies and the rest of the party felt the same.

I then sent the group back with Amy our steward at the time (for Ghost Experience Cymru) to the north gate via the external route. But the oddest things started to happen, time seemed to have shifted, I think my mind drifted. I then decided to head after the group.

Entering the field to the south of the gate, I started to have intrusive thoughts, along the lines that I felt I had been here for 5 years, even worse that my parents had died. I took a route towards my evening walks party, the same course I had only taken about 20 minutes earlier and got lost. I started to think I had lost everything and that my fiancée had also given up on me.

I eventually got back to the field, walked forward again, and have taken the original route; from a few moments ago, I arrived back at the front of the Priory. My group had gone, I couldn't hear anything; and my car had gone also, it was all true then, I had moved forward in time. Praying was the answer. The atmosphere changed. I could see my car again.

Then I found my group and I explained the story and experience. I did not want to go through that again.

THE WOODWOSE BEAST OF PETERSTON-SUPER-ELY

PETERSTON-SUPER-ELY

Peterston-Super-Ely is one of those village is the Vale of Glamorgan, that you just don't stumble across by accident, you have to go and find it. It even has its fair share of a castle, church, two pubs serving food: the Three Horseshoes Inn and The Sportsman Rest.

This is a great story from Alex Morgan. One night Alex was driving back from Cardiff with her friend; driving through Peterston Super Ely, and they were chatting in full conversation. Then they both saw something in the centre of the road, a human shape covered in hair from top to bottom. You would think that they would have at least stopped, or had some kind of panic attack, but they carried on talking, and didn't stop driving. Then about a minute later, they both said to each other, "did you just see that it was bigger than a dog?"

They believed it had to be a dog, but with the doubt settling in, there was a possibility it may have been something else, a lot more terrifying as it had a humanoid shape. They discussed about turning the car around to inspect, but didn't? Why was this, was it because it dawned on them that the creature in the road was something really abhorrent, against the laws of nature? They believe there was obviously something there.

Alex tells us that, "the thing was lying in a foetal position covered in masses of hair on the road. Both didn't acknowledge the hideous creature until they were driving away from the scene. The fact is, this is a familiar response.

Later on, they discussed the occurrence with a friend. The friend exclaimed this was the werewolf of Peterston super Ely, there had been several sittings. Should it be said that something this strange in the road should have been reported to the police? Or would ringing the police be placing you in for ridicule?

Moreover, should Alex and her friend have turned the car around to inspect? What would the reaction have been of the beast of Peterston-Super-Ely if they had faced it down?

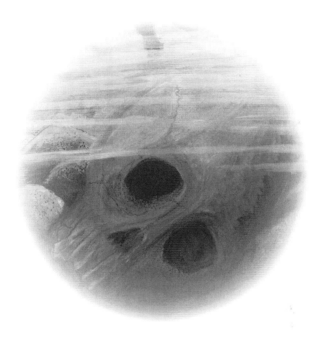

THE BOYS VILLAGE AT WEST ABERTHAW

ABERTHAW

West Aberthaw (Vale of Glamorgan) is just that the other half of the village on the West bank of the River Thaw. The Boys village was part of a network of holiday camps (as part of the Boys' Clubs of Wales network), established in the 1920s to offer the sons of miners a youth experience. The Boys village (sometimes referred to with the acronym St. Athan), was opened in 1925, and all operations had closed by 1990, with attempts of revival, but the site has slowly decayed and ill-treated since.

Simon Jenkins a resident of St. Athan, who offers this short but interesting story. A few years ago, Simon popped over to check out the boys village. He had been intrigued by history, and all the stories he had been told about strange goings on there.

Simon walked through the first building inside the complex. And this is the moment! As he got about halfway along the corridor, a wave of energy went past him, a bit like a breeze. He told us that although he felt the energy, the leaves and debris underfoot were not disturbed by this energy. Simon tells us that the energy definitely wasn't the wind.

You can image the reaction from Simon where he felt rather disturbed by this 'energy', and soon after he left the complex.

A BRONWYDD PARK GHOST STORY

PORTH

Bronwydd Park, Porth (Rhondda) was donated to the people (Rhondda Urban District Council) by William Evans in 1921, a wealthy manufacturer. Alongside a bowling green and tennis courts, two ornate entrances were built, a war memorial, pathways, planting of trees and a lot more.

This is part two of our look in this edition of Bronwydd Park. The short story of Jane in the evening in the dark. It was a moonlight night; we were sat there at the bench by the bowling green in the park. Until? So, after half an hour of absolute quietness, the end door of the shed that was definitely locked, and there was no noise from that shed at all.

The locked door that did not open after half an hour, there started banging very loudly from behind; all that time, on that door (that was being banged from the inside), and you could see the door moving almost fluid like. Jane got up and ran out of the park.

It wasn't till after Jane told the story to other people, she found out the park was haunted, and other people hung themselves there.

ST. QUINTIN'S CASTLE A VISION FROM THE PAST

LLANBLETHIAN

St. Quintin's castle, known also as Llanblethian, just Southwest of Cowbridge, is a spectacular gatehouse. The gatehouse is mainly all that remains of this once substantial site. The internal keep is very much in ruin, and forward Barbican all removed; but the curtain wall in the main does still stand. St. Quintin's was never completed by the De Clare family however. Alex had seen it one day as it was when it was built, a mirage from the past.

Alex Morgan tells us of passing St. Quintin's castle years ago. Alex had never seen the castle before. She remembered the castle looked amazing, not as a ruin, but as a full Medieval castle. A whitewashed wall, impressive gateway, and barbican (external castle defence tower), towers and curtain wall. She discussed at the time with her partner, about having some time to go back again.

Then years later, one day Alex was disappointed to see the castle was all in ruins. This she felt was not the same castle that she had seen. But on reporting this disappointment to her partner he said, "it had always been there, and it had always looked like that, 'spooky'."

But, Alex is still resolute, as far as she had known when she saw it in its entirety those years previous, she had seen it, as it was meant to be seen, when it had been built. Using this story in the book, was 50/50, then I realised, that something similar had happened to me, around 25 years ago. I had taken a group to visit the humps and bumps of the defences that existed at the Penycoedcae Roman fort (South of Pontypridd). I had pointed out the wrong earthworks to the group as representing the banks of the fort, only to be shown minutes later by historian Brian Davies, the actual bank. This was several metres high I felt at the time. In visiting the site years later, this tall bank, was nothing but a small rise in the field. Was I in-fact seeing its original height back 25 years ago, as it was meant to be?

A HAUNTED HOUSE

CARDIFF

Cardiff is steeped in history; it was in Llandaff that I first went on my first ghost walk with Jim. Cardiff has a huge presence on the ghost experience map, against a backdrop of the Romans, the Medieval and everything that came after. Not forgetting the many monks buried around the city at least three monasteries, echoes of war, the dark side of Victorian Cardiff, and its race riots.

We are not publishing the exact location, as she didn't want ghost hunters flocking to the house. But we are near to the centre of Cardiff. Sarah went to town on this piece, in her own words, "I'll just write down what I can think of". She grew up in a 1920s house along with my brother and sister. It was a happy house and she had never noticed anything strange until later in her years. Then it started, although Sarah and her sister would always run 3 stairs at a time, coming down the stairs as we always felt there was someone chasing us.

Sarah's friend and herself were sitting in the lounge watching TV on Boxing Day, and there was no one else in the house. They both heard footsteps walking across their parents' bedroom directly above, so immediately they went upstairs, and no one was there. Her other friend came to stay 'from away', and they were both getting ready to go clubbing, and she heard her chatting away to someone whilst she was getting ready in the bathroom. Sarah walked back into her bedroom, and she screamed, I said what's the matter, her friend said I thought I was talking to you whilst I had my head down blow drying her hair. My friend said, "you were stood in the doorway, and you had a pale blue dressing gown on and then suddenly the person walked away.

Then my friend said, "you walked in fully dressed to go out!" Sarah remembered that day clearly, there was no one living in the house that had a pale blue dressing gown. Sarah's mum and dad were sat eating downstairs at the kitchen table, my friend understandably didn't stay at our house again. How to lose friends? Go to Sarah's house.

There was another time that we had an electrician working in the basement of the house, and he heard footsteps walk across the kitchen floor. So, he went around to the front of the house as he wanted a cup of tea, but as he got to the front door my youngest sister was just putting her key in the door coming home from school. The electrician asked her if Sarah's mum was home as he fancied a cup of tea, but she said sorry no one is home until later, he didn't say anything as he didn't want to frighten her.

A boyfriend of Sarah's slept on the sofa one night and when she went down in the morning, he told Sarah that my dad had poked his head around the door, just as it was starting to get light as he had to be up very early in the morning for work. Sarah didn't think anything of it until that night, the family were sat down for dinner and Sarah said "oh dad, I see you saw Tom stayed over on the sofa last night", to which he replied "no I bloody well didn't know that", but Sarah said "well you must have as you poked your head around the door" and he said "good morning John, hope you don't mind me staying over". But this wasn't Sarah's dad, so we don't know who it was?

Another time Sarah's mum and dad went away on holiday and Sarah went to check the mail, and make sure the house was ok with her dog. Sarah unlocked the front door, and went into the porch, she picked up the post and then opened the door into the hall, but all of a sudden, her dog went mad barking and snarling. All her hackles were up, and she was just staring up the stairs. Sarah thought that they had been broken into, so she rang her brother and got him to come over and they went upstairs expecting to find the house done over but absolutely nothing. Sarah didn't check the house again for the duration of my parents' holiday, she got my husband to do it and he didn't believe in ghosts.

The next day her husband went to her parents' house, after he had opened the front door, it slammed behind him, with the key still in from the outside. He was locked in the porch, and he had to ask a person walking by if they could open the door for him from the outside. The next time he went, he couldn't open the door going into the hallway. The rug from over the other side of the large hallway was bunched up to the door, this stopped him from getting in. He just said it must have been a draft coming from the basement. and that this had moved the rug some 12ft across the hallway.

Sarah's next dog that she had some years later would never settle in the house, when she went to visit her mum and dad. Her dog would literally have to drag himself across the hallway to the kitchen, and he would be looking up the stairs. Her dog would just whine and whimper the whole time Sarah was there, so she stopped taking him there when she visited.

When Sarah's mum used to go away with her friends, her dad would hate staying in the house on his own and he used to say that if he fell asleep in the chair, he would wake up ice cold; and feel someone standing at the bottom of the stairs watching him. Then when he went upstairs, he felt someone was at the bottom of the stairs, but nothing ever happened to my mum.

Sarah's sister moved back in with their mum years later with her 2 daughters, and she hated turning off the lights and walking up the stairs. Her sister felt that she always felt very eerie and as if someone was watching her.

Sarah's brother visited my mum one day with his baby, who was about 10 months old and as he was leaving and chatting to my mum in the hall: My brother was aware that his little one suddenly turned his head to the side and was looking directly up the stairs as if looking at someone. His little one started to laugh and wave to someone at the top of the stairs. After all Sarah's brother who does not believe in ghosts, said he felt very uncomfortable and put his head down and left quickly.

Finally, Sarah's daughter some years ago stayed the night with her grandmother, and found herself around 3am in the kitchen downstairs in the pitch black holding an empty glass. She's never slept walked and is petrified of the dark, so just legged it back upstairs. And what a strange end to Sarah's stories at her childhood home.

A VERY BARRY GHOST STORY BURLINGTON STREET

BARRY

Much of Barry has changed over the past 130 years or more since the cutting of the first sod for the construction; and opening of the Barry Dock.

James Eddy tells us that in the early 2000s, that he was living in an old house in Burlington St, Barry with his wife and four-year-old daughter Marybeth.

At around 9pm one evening while sat in the living room watching TV, I saw someone moving on the stairs. Well obviously, James thought that their daughter had gotten out of bed, so James got up and walked out of the room to take her back to bed.

As James went through the door he turned and looked up the stairs, James saw a small girl in an old-style type of dress. He had only saw her for a second before she disappeared, but James did notice that the girl was about 12 years old. James and his wife caught glimpses of someone moving out of the corner of their eyes on several occasions; in the 10 years they lived in the house.

By taking note of those figures moving out of the corner of our eyes, we are always prone to seeing something special one time, keep watching.

MARCROSS MEDIEVAL CHURCH, A NEW LOOK ON AN OLD STORY

MARCROSS

Marcross (Vale of Glamorgan coast, Southeast of Wick) is rich in archaeological remains from all periods. Marcross played an important role in the medieval period, with its own fully operation monastic grange.

The ghost of the brother of a sailor who had died in the winter of 1588 at the time of the Spanish Armada. We won't print the full story here, as we believe in printing newly told and discovered stories in this series. But in short, the ghost gets a young gentleman to find bones of his brother, and then they are reburied by the boy in the churchyard at Marcross. But here is what one of our walkers at our Marcross event believes.

Here's what James Wilcock said about the ghost at Marcross graveyard: "When the young man dug up the bones and moved them into the graveyard, he didn't realise that the ghost had lied to him. The bones actually belonged to the ghost himself, but he didn't want to tell anyone why he wasn't buried in consecrated ground. The ghost needed someone to move his bones as this was the only way he could pass on and not be stuck here. The ghost made up the story about it being his brother's bones, so that someone would feel sorry for him and do what he asked."

We may now ask if James is correct in his assumption, then not being buried in holy ground could indicate that the ghost may have committed suicide as in life, or something much worse? Could he have been a criminal of terrible intent such as a murderer?

THE AMITYVILLE STORY OF DINAS POWYS

DINAS POWYS

Dinas Powys has a rich history, for one it boasts one of the finest still standing native build castles in Glamorgan. Did you know at one point at high tide 500 years ago most of lower Dinas Powys was under water?

A tragic story, "the witness" told by the Raven - her very own pain. The week before Christmas 2016 Ravens friend was living in the house at the bottom of the Gables, Dinas Powys. They went that week with the spirits of the day, happy Christmas shopping. On the return at dusk she said, "look at my house doesn't it look like the house of the Amityville horror?" Then Raven remarked, "oh no don't say that."

So then a week later the Raven repeated the experience of catching the train to Barry. This time they shopped on the high Street; having lunch, and she had her photograph taken with Father Christmas in a pub, we returned on the train once again. The two friends were in the lovely house; well not so lovely Amityville horror house as it turned out.

They were about to have some food and drink, and she was twinkling some Christmas decorations in the mirror. The poor lady turned to Raven and said,"Hey sweetie you know what I don't feel so good", at which point she suddenly collapsed into the Ravens arms and that was her passing away. Yes, Raven called the ambulance etc. The banshee has struck again, don't you think? Prior to that, during the week Raven had a dream, the visitation of the screaming banshee; she believed the Gwraich y Rhibyn was telling her that something close to her would pass into the next world. Then shortly and the deepest of sorrow, and so it did happen that way.

Oh and that picture with Santa Claus, his fist was above her head. Well, it looked that way, but not meant in a negative way. Her friend, she died of a brain aneurysm.

EVENTS AT TYLORSTOWN

TYLORSTOWN, RHONDDA

Tylorstown in the Rhondda Fach is named after Alfred Tylor; a geologist, who first came to the area in search of Black Gold. Tylor's claim of minerals rights saw the opening of the Pendyrus Colliery in 1872. And the rest as they say is history.

At Tylorstown, we meet Dean Drakes. In the street where Dean is living in now, is where he first lived there in his early 20s; before moving away and coming back. He used to live in number 14. Dean is a biker; he's got quite a few bikes, the house he's in now used be his old mates house (number 9). And the story is very much about is good old mate.

Back at the first time Dean lived at number 14, he had bought this old triumph; a 1958 model, that he has still got. Back in his early 20s, this guy came up the street; I didn't know him at the time, and he asked what I had under the tarpaulin. He said, "to put it in my garage, and don't leave it out here". So, I did what he asked, and we became mates.

Time went on, as time does, over a few years and Dean and his friend became good mates and I could go in his garage, he used to leave the door open for me and I used to tinker about on the bikes. Then Dean left his wife. He looked after the bike for Dean, for about 6 months and then Dean shifted it.

Years later Dean used to work for AMEX-Civil Engineering; a big firm, he worked in Barry as well. Dean had a phone call, as part of our team we had a job in the street where we are living now. They rang Dean up and asked him, "didn't you used to live in Tylorstown", and he said yes. They asked him what street, I said Edmunds Street. The company asked Dean, "did you know the bloke in number 9?", yes he said, "he was a good mate of mine". Then the mortal and sad words "Mike, hung himself on the weekend!" Dean as you can image was crushed.

Well years later, this house came up to let number 9. Dean had been living in a caravan over in Pentre in the back lane, he was working, and homeless.

Dean came over to the street and brought his son and took to show him where he used to go fishing. When he came back past the house, number 9, there was a 'To Let sign' on the house. Dean ended up having the house, he had been there for more than 13 years now. And for the first 7 years, the paranormal activity that went on, "well it was the best I've seen. Positive stuff it was my mate." He hung himself in the bedroom where I am now, now my bedroom. I lived with the spirit of my mate, for 7 years in this house, but he is gone now. And more of this story in book 3.

A NEW INSIGHT INTO A GHOST

MERTHYR MAWR

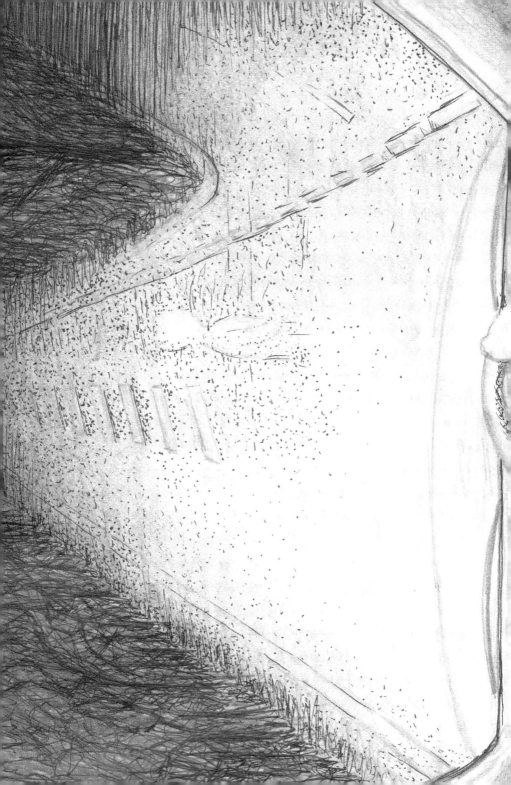

The landscape of Merthyr Mawr is exceedingly rich in ghost sightings. We see a rich tapestry of early Christian carved stones, alongside the earlier ghosts of Roman settlement. Then a landscape that breaths King Arthur, the old Kings of Glamorgan, and then Norman betrayal. For the darkness and light is always in contrast at Merthyr Mawr. Then the emboldened madness of the New Inn, and the complicit murdering of the unwary at the hands of the Nichols family.

This is a pretty creepy story especially when you're driving down towards the junction, to the Lane that leads to the house of horrors: The New Inn. A pitch-black lane. Nigel Nash shares his story, that is so amazing.

He once worked for Asda (Home shopping department), Bridgend and used to start work at 3.45am. Nigel would travel from Porthcawl to Bridgend, coming up 3 steep hill, down the tump and then past the roundabout; that takes you to Laleston. You are now on the road towards Bridgend; two lanes on the left and one on the right. Heading towards the junction off for Merthyr Mawr New Inn Road, a little small road. It was Summertime; cold, about 2 - 3 degrees. There were no other cars on the road, just myself. No reflections, lamps, or car head lights.

It happened just over 10 years ago, and Nigel will always remember it, as it occurred yesterday. A figure suddenly moved across the road, and there were no legs visible. It emerged from the wooded area of tree's (opposite New Inn Road) on left to right, heading towards the dark lane towards the Merthyr Mawr New Inn Road; towards the humped back bridge. Not at an extremely fast pace, but to get across the road as if it was in mortal flesh to avoid traffic. Nigel had a full view of entire area as it moved. Nigel had got the best look as he got closer and closer.

The figure was bright; so clear it was just the top half part of the body; the waste up, no legs. He was light in colour, neither white nor grey; so light silhouetted in the darkness, that Nigel could actually see him at that time in the morning.

There was no face, just the head shape and body. He was 5ft 10 well just under 6ft medium build, it was so clear. Not too cloudy at night, no moon on show - slightly overcast. There were still no other cars about with their headlights on, so there is no doubt this was really in front of Nigel, and he would never see it again.

Nigel mentioned it all to the guys in work what he had seen a month later (staff in Asda's). And the answers that came back was, "yes somebody did get knocked down in that area, a teenage lad". Whether there is a link, he hasn't thought more. And let's leave it there.

Nigel drove that road for 6 years, 3 of those years at exactly the same time. Nigel had tried to recreate that moment with the ghost. With car lights turned on and off, street-lamps, the same time, nothing could get that recreation to see the spirit perform again. Nigel even tried to fake a ghost with reflections, thinking of a photographic light leak into a lens on a printed picture, he couldn't get any of that to even come close to a ghost experience. But Nigel believes that he needed to go at the same time, conditions, and the second that originally had seen it and maybe you would see that man again?

THE SPIRIT AT THE LAY-BY

LLANMIHANGEL

Llanmihangel contains the most beautiful of lived in Manor houses in the Vale of Glamorgan. Opposite the manor you can also find one of two churches in the Vale that still do not have electricity, and there is a great hidden well near-by, with a carved face on it.

We have a story from a taxi driver. She was working in Cowbridge and was waiting outside the Manor House up in Llanmihangel. She was more or less just opposite the Manor in a little lay-by lane, that goes onto the field. As our taxi driver friend waited there, as it is very, very quiet there.

Whilst the taxi driver was sat there waiting, she looked forwards towards the manor. But with a side glance she could see in her mirrors something moving behind her, something white. She thought first of all it was sheep. But it wasn't the sheep, because she drove away from there. The driver was overcome with a feeling of fear and trepidation.

In turning the car around to look back at the spot, with her headlights on, there was nothing there at that stage. The taxi driver is convinced in thinking that there was something there definitely, but what type of entity for now, we do not know.

A STORY OF FOOTSTEPS

LLANDAFF NORTH

Llandaff has a rich history of multiple ghost sightings. Alongside the River Taff, the secrets within the mist have much to tell us, for we turn to a story near the 'weir'.

James Wilcock tells us an interesting story from Riverview near to the weir. When he was about 7 years old; when he used to live on the second floor of his house in Llandaff North, he tells us about the footsteps.

My great grand-dad used to live at Riverview, and passed away when he was around 5 years old. He can remember once when he was little; whilst nodding off to sleep, he could hear footsteps and he always used to think it was his beloved dad. The footsteps were of comfort at night.

One night James was a little restless, and on hearing the footsteps, James decided to investigate. James went to talk with the person whose footsteps he had heard. James slowly opened the door of his room, poking his head around the corner, and witnessed there was no-one there. The footsteps obviously headed towards his dad's room. So, James went to his dad's bedroom, and when James opened the door, he noticed that his dad was fast asleep. So, thinking logically James thought it must have been someone else. But there was problem with that assumption however, no one else was in the house.

When James was 8, whilst on the ground floor by the kitchen he could hear a name being called out. This was no unfamiliar name, but it was in fact James name being repeated. The voice went "James, James, James, James…" it was a mature voice calling his name. James in the moment thought it may have been a nightmare and not real, but then he realised that the sun was coming up and it wasn't a dream he was wide awake; this actually happened.

A GHOST IN A TRAILER

CULVERHOUSE CROSS

Culverhouse Cross is the home to the Victorian underground railway tunnel, which is still partially accessible, if you like getting muddy. Also, the Roman road, that heads out of Cardiff, known as the Julia Maritima (coastal Roman road) that passes this way.

This story of Nathan takes us back to the mid -1990s. The year was 1996 and Nathan had moved into a trailer, at the Culverhouse Cross Cambria Trailer Park, and after a while ghostly happenings started, I lived there for 12 years. Nathan left the Trailer Park 13 years ago.

A woman that Nathan used to live with there was into her regression. She used this skill to past life regress him. On one occasion and maybe more, whatever energies had been around due to this, created some kind of entity. These entities were gone when she moved out.

However, but before she moved out, the energies had manifested. Nathan tells us his cat misty, was sensitive. When he would call her from the bedroom to the living room, in the trailer my cat would react. Part way along the distance between the two spaces (bedroom, then bathroom, then kitchen doorway and living room) her pace would increase at the kitchen doorway; where you would go into that space, then slow down when she got to me, every-time. Nathan would always used to see something, at the spot where the cat would speed up. There was an entity that was 2ft tall that I could see out of the corner of my eye, and sometimes full on and always at that kitchen doorway. The little entity left with Nathan's then ex-girlfriend.

The question must be, what is this entity, what does it represent?

A STORY OF A PHANTOM WEDDING

COWBRIDGE

The Duke of Wellington public house in Cowbridge, is known as the place of the hauntings of the Grey Lady and is one of the surviving such establishments amongst more than 20 that had once served the population of Cowbridge, with its favourite alcoholic beverage.

This story takes us to the Duke of Wellington 16 years ago. Many years ago, Alex Morgan was in the Duke of Wellington with her daughter, who was about 4 at the time. There party was sat upstairs. There was a door ajar adjacent to the room that we were in. Her daughter you could say was very curious about everything. Her daughter was milling about, and she would go up and down the room, then in and out into the corridor.

The curiosity got to her, she had to go and look into that room where the door was ajar. She came back in, and said, "I can see people dancing in there, and there is a lady with a white ball gown on." Not so much a vivid imagination, but her daughter described the gown to 'T', she said it was "like a wedding dress". It was a Saturday afternoon, but there were not any functions on or anything else like that; usually there would be a party using that room. Then when we were leaving, we could see that it was an empty function room. This was a place that people could have been dancing in the past and used as a ball room.

NORTH CLIFF DOCK BEACH

PENARTH

North Cliff Dock beach is a term used by some to describe a location of beach just South of Penarth head and the entrance to the old port of Penarth.

The Raven takes a visit to North Cliff Dock beach Penarth, going back a few years. Raven happily walks along the North Cliff Dock beach, at half tide; there is a bit of mud, old logs, and things sticking out of the mud. As she was walking along, she suddenly stopped, and there it was! There was a creature, and Raven exclaimed, "owe, hello I didn't see you there?"

And there was this creature, that looked at me, and transmogrified into a log, that held some bladderwrack. Not a traditional female mermaid. Raven believes that it was a type of Mermaid. It was a dark toned mermaid, that was fittingly complementary with its surroundings. Obviously the mermaid did not want to be seen, and Raven had taken it with great surprise, and that exchange took place. Not to intrude on each others space, Raven carried on with her merry way.

THE FATE OF BILLY PARROCK

GILESTON

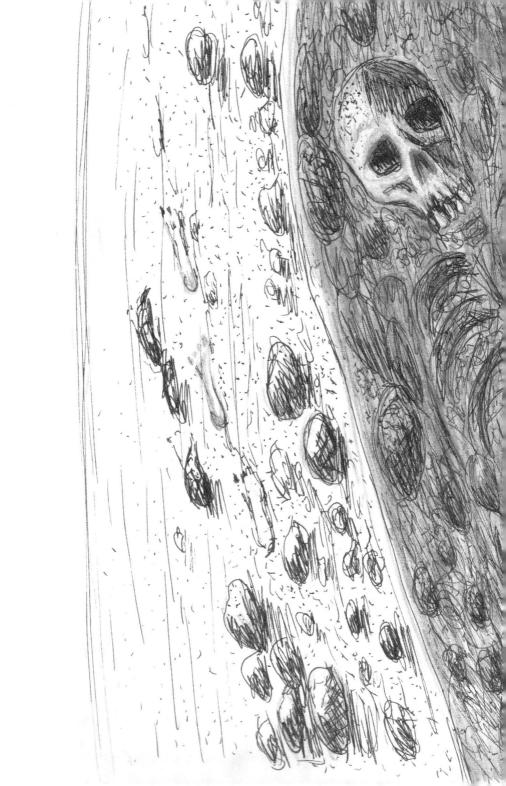

Research by Richard Enos. We delve into a strange and dark landscape, that of Gileston. A village with a medieval manor, it's church and olde worlde buildings. A site that would have played a vital role in defending our coast, a huge line of concrete blocks, to guard against Hitler's tanks still dominate the landscape.

We have taken a different direction with this piece. Richard Enos has helped with the research for this piece - well all of it, I have just interpreted it, thanks Dicky. He delved into, 'The Cardiff Times' of the 22nd September 1906, with the headline Aberthaw Skeleton buried in sand and pebbles. It all relates to the mysterious disappearance of Billy Parrock, some bones, dreams, and ghosts.

Human remains had been found and thus reported. The elderly inhabitants of the Gileston and St. Athan villages remember the events of up to 60 years ago, at the Leys (Gileston). The events of that time are reported in the local media of the time, were based on vivid accounts, although a little impaired at times - it had been a long time ago for them. Were the bones found, actually those of the missing Billy Parrock? Could one of these elderly inhabitants be connected with the potential murder of Billy?

The reporter for this news, and one of a small elite, had interviewed three inhabitants (74, 75 and 78). There were slight discrepancies with their stories. Billy's sister had dreams of her brother. Mrs Gould; was her married name, but never got to be interviewed (as she was long since dead); residing at St Athan village. She dreamt that one night, she saw Billy buried in the sand and pebbles on the shore. The family all put their mind on it in the daytime, and dreamt about it at night, I suppose, and they insisted upon saying that he was buried in the sand. Billy also had a brother and another sister residing at the time in Llantwit Major, and a sister is supposed to still be living in Broughton near Wick.

The family took to excavating at the sand tumps; there were many, and not one missed the shovel. Nothing! The legendary Llantwit Major boys would turn up alas with the St. Athan boys to help; and sometimes, when both set of boys met together in the pubs of the area would quarrel.

Who was this apparent murdered victim: William David, a bachelor, who was known by the sobriquet as " Billy Parrock," through having been born at Parrock near Boverton. David they all agreed, was at the time of his disappearance employed my Mr D Davies Batsleys Farm. Grandfather of a certain Mr J. A. Davies, Eglwys Brewis Farm near St Athan, his occupation being that of a farm labourer. But he had a sideline, he occasionally assisted as one of the crew of the smack Picton, an old vessel which used to carry limestone to Cardiff.

One of those interviewed was a certain Mr William Thomas of Elm Cottage, St Athan, brother of the late Captain Thomas; who for many years lived at the Ocean House Hotel and is now 78 years of age. William was still very active and keenly intelligent and considered the exact time about 57 years ago when David disappeared ."It was always known that he was murdered (said Mr Thomas with emphasis), but there was not a scrap nor a scrip of the man to be found anywhere. It happened on a Sunday night in the autumn. The old Picton was on the pebbles and Billy was working on the vessel. At that time the only public-houses were the Ship Hotel and the Limpet. The Ship was always called the ' Leys.' The Ocean House had not been built at that time. In those days you could have a beer at any time night or day, Sundays or weekdays."

Billy had been seen in the Leys public-house and had some beer. A small boat was on top of the pebbles ready for him to go aboard the vessel, and the very next morning the boat was missing as well as Billy. Others left the public-house on this night the same time, and some of these said they saw Billy go off in the boat. And next morning there were the marks of footprints near where the boat had been on the pebbles. There was no police search, for there was only one policeman at Bridgend, and another- Thomas Thomas, or Twmmy Calchwr (Tom the Limeman), and he was at Cowbridge. At the time there was a hue and cry, and Llantwit boys came over, and they searched the shore, walking for miles to try and get a clue. Nothing!

Mr John Deere, Higher End, St Athan who is 74 years of age said he also remembered the main incidents, and how everybody was convinced at the time that Billy was murdered. "I knew Billy well," he continued. "He was a fine broad set man, about 6ft high, and was engaged on the farms in driving Oxen. They said at the time, that whoever killed him, sent the boat adrift down Channel in order to allay suspicion."

William Hopkins: a mason of Gileston, said he was engaged years later in building the Ocean House, and a wall was built within a few feet to where the body was later found. It was strange (he said) that nothing was discovered at the time. "I fix the date as being 59 years ago, because I was then 15 or 16 years of age and was employed occasionally by Mr Thomas Jenkins in weeding his garden near the Ship." Could William be telling us that the body that was found was not Billy's, as it postdates the Ocean House and not the death of Billy. Or now this is a suggestion? William had known all along that Billy was buried there, and simply didn't rediscover it whilst building the Ocean House. What am I suggesting?

Finally, we need a ghost, this is a ghost book after all. The Leys Ghost, "There was also talk of a ghost?"

"Oh aye (and the old man's eyes brightened up: William Hopkins eyes!), many times men on the boats were afraid to go on deck at the Leys in the night, because they said they had seen the ghost of a man with his head off."
What a strange end. Rest in peace Billy Parrock.

A ROMAN GHOST

LLANDOUGH

Llandough once held the remains of one of few known Roman Villa's in the whole of South Glamorgan, but now since demolished for a housing development. In the church graveyard still is the IRBIC cross re-erected out of 4 separate monuments, with the base carved stone from the Roman Villa that once was.

In the early 1990s, Raven would visit her friend with her son; and Ravens daughter, at the flats at Corinthian Close (near to St. Dochdwy's church, Llandough); they had not been standing long. Raven and her friend would be sat there chatting over a cup of tea. It would always be a Sunday to see her friend there every week. Then suddenly a little girl would appear playing with a ball running through the room. Every-time we would just say, "there goes the little girl again".

Raven being a believer in ghosts never thought anything much of it. That's what she would see. Until years later then Raven found out about the extensive Roman period burial site at the rear of St. Dochdwy's church. The girl wore some kind of dress and was around the age of 3 or 4 years old; a happy child; a playful child. Both the adults, and maybe there two children would be aware of her presence and let her play.

Corinthian close as point of fact was construction on the Roman Villa site, excavated by the Glamorgan-Gwent Archaeological Trust in the late 1970s. It was the politicians of the day who allowed the site to be destroyed and not the developer. Could it have been a Roman ghost of a happy girl, who may have died tragically from an accident? As few buildings had been built at the site between the late Roman period 450s, and the late 1500s, I have no other suggestion who the ghost of the girl actually may be, but Roman is a useful suggestion.

Raven believes that the ghost was a benevolent spirit, and just wanted to play with their children. Now that is a lovely story and was the last one, I edited to be in this book. This story is where I completed the book and sent it to be proofread - Jess.

A GHOST WALKING AT RAF ST ATHAN

ST ATHAN

Although RAF St. Athan is known as an extensive airbase, we have something else that was once extensive. In the prehistoric period there is extensive discussion, that 100s of burial mounds and monuments were levelled to create the airfield and other structures. But more relevance to the airfield again, there it is rumoured that there are aircraft flat packed and crated dumped in holes in the ground; unopened, littered around the confines of the site. Metal Detectors eat your hearts out but watch out for un-exploded bombs.

This is a further story thanks to James Eddy. Whilst James and his wife lived in their married quarter at RAF St Athan, a couple of strange things happened. One was while James wife was having a bath; she had the door open, and the lights were off on the landing; and she could see across the landing onto the stairs. James was on the other hand, watching TV in the lounge and the door was closed.

Just before James wife got out of the bath, she noticed a shadowy figure stood on the stairs, and it looked like it was just standing there looking at her. James wife called out thinking that it was him, and it just stayed there. James wife started shouting and he heard her, and he came out of the lounge. As he opened the door and the light from the lounge went out onto the stairs the figure disappeared.

Ow that is spooky, I'm sure anyone would have reacted the same. Thanks James.

THE BURTONS GHOST OF BARGOED PART I

BARGOED

Burtons in Bargoed is still open, and it makes great reading. A town that became prominent in regard to coal mining.

The Burton's Ghost of Bargoed is told to us today by Jeffrey. It was about the early 1970s Jeffrey was working in Bargoed Burtons; the Taylors. It was a Monday morning, at the time most of the staff were doing the books from the previous weekend, because it was always busy. So, he was working by himself; but another staff member was nearby, Jeffrey was watching the door: in case anyone came in. In those days you had to pounce upon them, to see if they wanted to buy anything.

Jeffrey was working, then he glanced up, he then saw a guy coming in through the front door of the shop. So, when he had put his pen down and looked up there was nobody there? It was quite a big shop at the time, Jeffrey decided to investigate to see if he was behind those some big thick pillars; there was no sign of him, he looked around the store. Jeffrey thought he may have gone to look at the window display, no sign, then Jeffrey thought he may have gone somewhere else in the store.

Also, his elder brother who was working in the store at the same time as me, Jeffrey asked him the following, "Col did you see a guy coming through the door, by there?" He said no, and Jeffrey thought that was strange. Jeffrey's brother asked him, "what did he look like?" Jeffrey's description was, that the man wore standard clothes of the time, he was quite a tall guy and was wearing a hat; used in the 70s, an oldish guy, and under his arm he had some firewood. My brother Colin said, "bloody hell it sounds like the guy who we used to call Pop Palmer. Pop worked in the Bargoed pit, and he had retired. But came out of his retirement occasionally and would work in Burtons on the weekend; as a Saturday salesman in the early 1970s".

Colin remembered that Pop on a Monday morning every week would go into the canteen at the Bargoed pit for a cup of tea. They were okay with it after he'd retired; because he knew all the staff and he would always go home with some wood for his fire. So, Jeffrey said, "I couldn't believe it when my brother told me what happened to pop Palmer?"

Jeffrey's brother told him what happened to Pop. At one time they asked if Pop would go to Ebbw Vale and work in Burton's branch; to act as relief as they were short staffed. Then tragedy struck, apparently Pop got off the bus in Ebbw Vale and a person in a car killed Pop outright.

The ghost of Pop a little lost still visits his old store in Bargoed, wondering what had happened!

A PIXIE AND THE GREAT GRANDPARENTS

NORTH CORNELLY

North Cornelly today, is slowly being seen as a outer district of Porthcawl. But North Cornelly has its fair share of being a product of Norman control in the area, and its association Sturmi (Stormy) family.

Ceri-Elaine Barnes offers us a story and "my goodness" it is worthwhile reading! Ceri-Elaine was born in what was the last house in North Cornelly, on Heol Fach, at the side of the house were the fields going up to the sand dunes.

Ceri-Elaine used to see things as a child - as you do!! One day she was sitting playing on the floor; while her mam sat on the settee knitting, and in walked a pixie like creature. Now that must have been amazing to see. She watched him walk in from the kitchen, across the room, then realised that Ceri-Elaine was actually watching him.

The pixie started jumping up and down in a real temper, shouting at Ceri-Elaine. She just continued to look at him, he then turned and walked back towards the kitchen, and started jumping up and down in anger at her again and stormed off. It was only the turn of the 2000's that Ceri-Elaine told her mam about it. This was after we visited a cousin of hers who showed her photos of her great grandmother and great grandfather.

She had to bite her tongue to stop herself exclaiming at first sight of the photo "I know him!" But it was such a strange moment, as Ceri-Elaine recognised him as the man who used to sit in the armchair, smiling lovingly at her as she played, this would be up to the age of seven before she moved up to where she lives now. Ceri-Elaine now has some interesting copies of the photos mentioned above. One night she was looking out of her bedroom window, towards the sand dunes and saw a flaming torchlight procession in the distance. She learnt years later that they used to do that for ancient funerals! I rarely mention these experiences! A phantom funeral is what Ceri-Elaine is referring to here. Phantom funerals were seen as a portent of your own death: a Memento Mori. However, at such a young age the rules of such whilst Ceri-Elaine watched the 'ancient funerals, must have been dispensed with as she is very much alive.

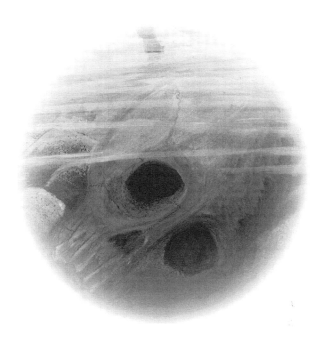

A GHOST IN THE ROOM

ABERTHAW

East Aberthaw is a village on the coast on the east bank of the River Thaw. There are myths, legends and ghosts abound, and this story certainly adds to that.

When Steve (he is 64 now) was only 5 or 6 years old, he is convinced to this day that he saw a ghost on two separate occasions; in the house where he lived at East Aberthaw (Vale of Glamorgan). The house is directly opposite the East Aberthaw railway signal box and occurred about 59 years ago.

On both occasions the ghostly figure appeared on the wall in my bedroom upstairs. There was no sound or changes in atmosphere. The details of both images were seemingly drawn out onto the wall; that consisted of thick bright, white lines, like thick chalk. The first image that Steve remembers seeing was of a life-sized boy in short trousers, this must have been alarming enough for Steve as a young boy to see in his house. But then we have the second image, and obviously more terrifying than the first, that of a very large head of a woman with distinct curly hair. I can't image the fear that Steve must have felt as a young boy. My own mum is terrifying enough, turning the lights out in my bedroom when I was a child, think of a stranger just appearing?

The image of the boy was just there when Steve looked at the wall (diving under the blankets in fright and then peeping to see if it had gone). The strange events associated with the second image are bizarre to say the least. The woman's head appeared first as a bright white dot, which rapidly drew out into the head in front of him. In Steve's own words, "man I was scared (again diving under the blankets)".

Was this Steve's childhood imagination gone wild after watching a Black and White (there was never any colour) version of The Twilight Zone; originally broadcast in the 1960s? It seems Steve has no doubt this was real, he can vividly remember those two occasions as if it happened yesterday. Furthermore, there may have been a second witness.

When Steve was a boy, he was sharing a bed with his younger brother. His brother also kept diving under the blankets after seeing both images. I'm sure Steve recanted that his brother had said that he'd seen it too, "although he may have just said that; because I'd mentioned it to my parents, and he didn't want to be left out. I'm not really in touch with him any-more, although I will ask him about it if ever I get the chance".

Steve felt that this story may have been too far-fetched for us to place into print, but funnily enough I disagree. What a great story.

WENVOE NURSING HOME

WENVOE

Did you know Wenvoe used to be on the route of a train line, with its very own station? There are many mysteries still hidden in Wenvoe awaiting to be found.

Nathan Williams tells of a friend who worked at a Wenvoe nursing home. My friend was painting and decorating at the Nursing home. He went into one of the rooms, it was empty, of particular interest in the room was a mirror, that was held in a frame. The frame allowed the mirror to be horizontally adjusted, 360 degrees. This same mirror was spinning, obviously my friend was alarmed by this.

We have chosen not to identify the exact location of the nursing home, as not to distress residents. The same nursing home was once a children's home, and many a life had been taken in an awful fire. The spinning mirror is not the only account of strange happenings at the nursing home.

I can image that many spirits may linger at a nursing home, and may those spirits eventually rest in peace.

AN ENTITY

PENRHYS

In the old Mid Glamorgan, the answer to the building housing crisis in the Rhondda was to build an estate on the top of a hill, far away from shops, and the train link. The Penrhys Housing Estate was completed by 1968 with 951 houses, its own police station, shop, and school. But things slowly went wrong, and the estate became notorious, with all but 300 houses demolished in the 1990s; but many like me see that its negative tag isn't totally deserved.

Martyn Davies starts off by telling us that the building with the blue roof, at the Penrhys housing estate, was not set up as a leisure centre or a supermarket in the 1960s but was the boiler house, for supplying hot water to the estate, and heating. The houses with the hottest water and central heating were those at the top, and the housing towards the bottom of the estate towards the Penrhys statute suffered the most.

Martyn tells us that in-front of the boiler house on a patch of now green grass towards the left-hand side, houses used to be there. Martyn used to live there. He tells us at 315 Heol Pendyrus, at his parents' home, as a child of 5 or 6 years old he used to clearly see white lights floating around his bedroom; which Martyn understands now as orbs. These round shaped orbs he used to see flowed fast around the bedroom going in a horizontal formation in-front of Martyn, and then going up and down, Martyn tells us he could not understand at the time what they were.

Martyn went into more detail about these orbs. They were small lights floating around the bedroom, some would be floating towards the ceiling, then bouncing up and down from floor to ceiling, 2 or 3 in the bedroom at a time, he believes this could have gone on for years. Laying in the bed of his bedroom watching lights flying around the bedroom would be all Martyn would see, then on different nights he would see a man outside the door. This must have been scary for a young boy; I certainly would have been petrified.

And Martyn clearly remembered seeing, "a white figure dressed in old type clothing and an old type of hat standing on his landing and with him waving to me", smiling and he seemed happy. It wasn't a monk, but a man it was in old type clothing, 1600s period maybe. Martyn used to lay on his side of his bed at the age of 5 or 6 years of age looking out of the door, wide awake seeing this happy entity, night after night. What a brave boy Martyn was not frightened at all, a kind spirit he could trust, nice!

Martyn believes that the reason for this activity was because of the Penrhys Geological fault. This fault runs from the ridge at Penrhys down the side of the mountain, left of the boiler house, skirting the estate. Then out of that fault comes, directly underneath the holy well at St. Mary's (Ffynnon Fair); this special site is actually on the fault line, that's why the spring water comes to the surface. This is called 'Telluric Energy' (earth energies), and studies have shown that these energies; and according to Martyn; will make spectres or spooks to materialise, so there is a lot going on at Penrhys.

Martyn tells us also that with this fault, and all the other activity, that Penrhys is a hive of energy: an ancient battle, a number of burial grounds throughout the periods, a monastery, the place of a grand medieval eisteddfod and so much more. The area of Martyn's house is a place on old Ordnance Survey maps marked as 'Erw Beddau', and 'Site of Battle. Marked on the maps of the past are also several burial mounds marked.

ROMAN ROAD

ST HILARY

We have undertaken a number of ghost walks, and held haunted evenings at the length of Roman Road at St. Hilary. The St. Hilary clump (the highpoint overlooking Cowbridge) is the place of a hanging tree, many a life has been sent to its end there. The Roman Road still survives as an eroded straight track alignment, with a drainage ditch.

A short experience story comes via James Wilcock, who had taken part on a Ghost walk with us (Ghost Experience Cymru). As James was standing by a very tall tree that flanks the road at Cowbridge, he had a feeling that something was amiss.

James tells us of a hand that came out and touched him on his shoulders. On looking behind there was nothing behind him. James describes the scene behind him. There was nothing except for dark shaded leaves, trees, and bushes. James tells us, "It felt as if someone had been walking past, in a little bit of a rush, a 2 second feeling then it was over".

From the Roman Road ghost evenings, we have experienced several sightings, feelings, and other experiences.

THE BURTONS GHOST OF BARGOED PART II

BARGOED

Bargoed may have derived from the ancient Cymraeg word of Bargod, meaning border or boundary. However, there is some discussion that from the 1500s, the word Bargoed, had mutated into meaning the boundary with the wood, as coed in Cymraeg means woodland.

Jeffrey's brother Colin's experience of a ghost. Jeffrey's brother told him of his experience up at Bargoed Burton's. When his brother went up the stairs to go to the next level in the store; into the very large office, surrounded by glass. By the side was the stairs, going up to the next level. He was on his own in the shop, but he felt a chill and he felt that there was someone standing behind him. He could sense something, and feel the hairs go up on the back of his neck, he turned round and there was nothing there, and that freaked him out.

Then another story, that was a couple of years later on. There was a young manager called Pat Moran; and he was a Catholic. We would usually finish at 6 o'clock on a Saturday, we would all go home but the manager would stay in the office doing some bookwork. The lights would be out in the shop except for the office.

The manager was doing the books, there was all glass around the office, and he looked up and he could see something walk upstairs. Pat went around and asked the person, "excuse me sir can I help you?" Nobody was there the shop was locked up, so there was no way anyone could get in and this freaked him out; and that from a religious man.

There you are, three strange occurrences, in Bargoed Burton's.

THE CHURCH GHOST

COWBRIDGE

Holy Cross Cowbridge, is highly unusual in that the Chancel is facing North, as most churches face East towards Jerusalem. Our story is proof that ghosts do exist and when photographed, the evidence is irrefutable.

It is very rare that footage has ever been forthcoming in regard to ghost sightings. On one occasion we do have photographic proof. At the beginning of our ghost walking series, back in 2015, a photo came our way. Whilst delivering leaflets, Michelle was suddenly called back to the house owner in Cowbridge and asked to look at an image that Michael Austin had taken not so long ago. The back story is that Michael had been out on a dark evening, taking photos of the principle Cowbridge church of Holy Cross. On returning, a ghostly figure is seen at attention silhouetted against the tower constructed in the early years on the 1400s. There had been nobody in the church graveyard at the time.

We have undertaken the excesses of exercise, to reproduce the image using light available at night, and using other props, with no avail. After this course of enquiry, and we are instructed Michael Austin has undertaken the same exercise, we are convinced this is a genuine sighting and photograph.

The figure is that seemingly of a soldier, with his back facing the tower looking into a Southerly direction towards the porch. His neck is slightly reclined, as if relaxing and pensive. The figure is stylishly donning a Mark I John Leopold Brodie 'Tin hat', issued to the British army after 1916 and used into the Second World War and beyond. Are the thoughts that enter our soldier those of regret, longing, or may be as some have said on guard duty, and waiting his next fag break? Who knows, maybe if you see the man again, ask him this question, "In god's name how may I be of some assistance?"

MORE GHOSTS FROM PENRHYS

PENRHYS

Penrhys is an ancient diverse landscape. We see of Penrhys its Prehistoric past, even links with the Roman period of occupation, then you could say the early times of Christianity and the legends of Arthur and the time of the Kings of Glamorgan. But moreover, the stories of its monks dominate.

Another story from Dean Drakes with his days at Penrhys, and the police legend John McPhail. Dean Drakes recites this story that he tells us is also from John McPhail. Starting at the Penrhys St. Mary's statue car park; at the top of the hill by the roundabout. Dean speaks to us, "as if you were walking from the statue towards the golf course, there used to be a part of a wall; however, this is knocked down and gone now. Before the old hospital, facing Northeast up towards the parish road, the wall would have been on the right. The base of the wall is the original monastery boundary wall. The original road is from years and years ago."

John told Dean of, "two monks and the estate reeve (not an abbot but a higher up monk). The top half of their torso's have been seen travelling through that road and down to St. Mary's well. Finally, many of us used to go 'Lamping' (to go rabbiting) at the Penrhys golf course. With my friends at night, we used to be in Competition with our lurches, and many strange things used to happen. I am sensitive and used to feel a lot of negative energy at penrhys."

This band of 'brothers' were here to cleanse the estate of the negative energies and in response to various happenings; a special religious event took place. Dean tells us, "And one time, they had the site blessed, a priest or a vicar walked around the site up Heol Pendyrus, and back around again. They were saying prays, an exorcism right, and they used holy water."

It is also said that the energies at Penrhys are because of the geological fault. We have mentioned that previous in this book. Dean mentioned, "that there was a lot of trouble and violence: a place used to put all social rejects at one time 70 and 80s, and it was like a war ground once, but with all that surprisingly it was still a lovely place." Now the Penrhys Estate has put behind it's past, and it can be a quiet place, set now with in the mysteries of time. And the people living there are lovely. For me the area around the boiler house has an energy!

THE STORY OF ELM GROVE ROAD

DINAS POWYS

The old Thatched Bay Tree cottage at Elm Grove looked very reminiscent in its heyday of those many cottages with thatch that used to exist across the Vale of Glamorgan in the early years of the 1900s. This cottage is no longer thatched in Dinas Powys; in fact, it was replaced entirely. There are one or two that see a new bit of thatching each year in the Vale of Glamorgan, a recent example is in Barry at Cold Knap farm.

The story of the Elm Grove Road ghost is a brief one, it is told by Raven. Raven bought the house at Elm Grove Road just over 10 years ago. The house that she now lives in with her husband; used to be one house (Bay Tree cottage), with numbers 11 and 13 built in its place. It used to be called Bay Tree Cottage, and it is believed had been owned by the same family for about 500 years. The remnant of the cottage that is fitting, is a Bay Tree that has grown between the two cottages in the garden ever since.

Tragedy struck the cottage in 1925, the thatch roof caught fire; apparently from a firework, in short, the cottage was raised to the ground. All that history gone in an instant. The Lady who lived here got out, with her black cat, and 2 medals from World War One awarded to members of the Peachy Lewis family. Two of which died at the Battle of the Somme: Gunner Frank Peachey aged 25, and Corporal John Peachey Lewis aged 32.

Raven and her husband were aware of a female presence round and about the home, and it was felt that the Lady of the house who left in 1925, was the mother. Maybe it would be best to walk with her to the War Memorial in Dinas Powys on Remembrance Sunday.

In 2013 Ravens husband was asked whether he could still feel the lady's presence? Ravens husband would strongly walk her up to the memorial in the morning of Remembrance Sunday in 2013, it was decided. Raven asked her husband, "can you feel her?" Although he wasn't sure Ravens husband did not disappoint.

Tom walked with the lady the next day with his naval uniform up to the War memorial. The Raven and Tom have not seen from her since. This was the walk she needed to take to be with her boys, now happily released from this realm; and that is what she did.

THINGS THAT HAPPEN: AN ITEM THAT WAS MEANT TO ARRIVE

ST ATHAN

This story takes place at RAF St. Athan, but the nature of the subject matter is intriguing. Like James I used to collect cigarette collector cards; they were everywhere when I was a child and did well out of the items that I collected them for, although I never smoked. Unfortunately encouraging people to smoke is not the done thing these days; hence no bonus cards.

A final story by James Eddy in this edition. The other thing that happened to James in the house at RAF St Athan, was while he used to smoke and collect cards from the cigarette packets. The cards he collected would be to send them off to get things like T-shirts and lighters; all with the cigarette companies name on them. He had collected for ages; to get a lighter, and when he had collected enough cards, he sent off for it.

About two weeks later sadly he got an envelope back with all his cards in, saying that they no longer did the collector thing. James as any would be, was really angry about it for most of the day.

Then night arrived while he was sat in the living room, he heard a loud crash from the back garden, so he went out to see what it was, just outside the patio doors. For on the patio table was sat a lighter stood upright, and when he picked it up, he saw it was the exact lighter that he had been saving up for.

James total faith my friend, maybe this all happened to tell you to stop smoking, and you also ended up with a lighter, result!

A RECORDED VOICE

EWENNY

Ewenny, may have a deep and mystical Medieval history, but what about before that? It has long been argued by some historians and archaeologists, that the Roman site of Bovium (Bomium) isn't in fact at Cowbridge, but directly underneath the current medieval walls at Ewenny. It has long been argued, in either case that this is the crossing point of the Julia Maritima. This Roman Road departs the A48 at the Golden Mile, heading through Corntown, with a detour through the Priory at Ewenny and then over the River Ewenny.

We see us at Ewenny again briefly. This time in the company of Randy Mandy, Dapple John, Facebook Mike and Horsegirl Liz. It was a haunted night, and around 12 midnight, I entered the North gatehouse, and started address spirit. Addressing spirit, takes the form of addressing verbal questions into the night. At this time in the winter months of 2016, I started asking questions such as these:

Where do you come from?

Who are you?

What are you doing here?

Well Randy Mandy stayed with me in the tower, with the tape-recording device on her mobile phone. She heard nothing that night until she got home.

The answer was heard on the recording to the last question as:

Etu

In other words, the answer 'etu' in Latin French (Norman), means 'and you'. The spirit had put the question back at me. It isn't the first time we have recorded 'spirit', but this clearly places the question at me, 'what are you doing here?" The mysteries of ghosts, and ghost detecting?

EDITION THREE WE VISIT

COLDKNAP
Dean Drakes and I discuss an energy spot

RHIGOS MOUNTAIN HAUNTING
The lady who appears in the middle of the road

THE GWRACH Y RHIBYN
The Gwrach strikes again in Dinas Powys

STAV'S MYSTERY
The man with greaves

And so much more...

Have you a genuine story for us?

GET IN TOUCH

karljlangford@hotmail.com

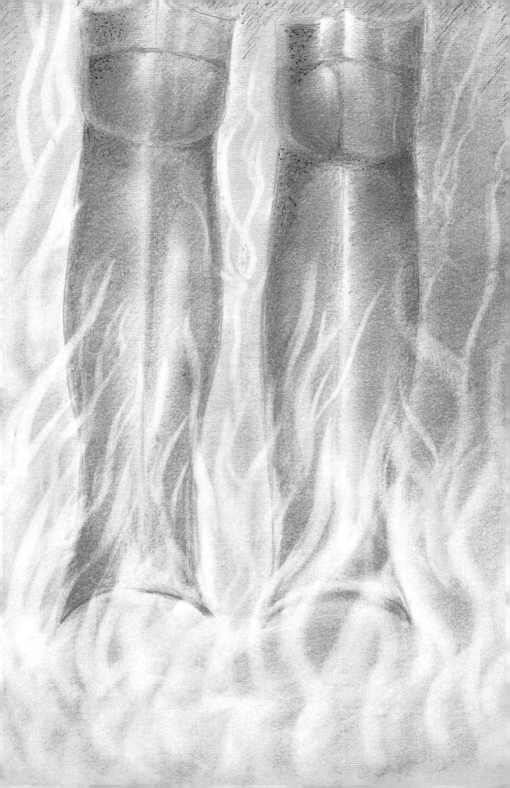